And When There Was No Crawdad, We Ate Sand

I0528730

Poems by

The NÜ Profits of P/o/e/t/i/c Di$chord

OAC
PRESS
OSAGE ARTS COMMUNITY

OAC Books
Belle, MO
osageac.org

OAC
PRESS
OSAGE ARTS COMMUNITY

Acknowledgments:

Special thanks to the editors of these publications:

Jason Ryberg: *Thimble Lit, Big Windows Review, Poetry Pacific Magazine, MyrtleHaus Magazine, Ink Pantry, Corvus Review, Five Fleas, Ink, Sweat and Tears, A Thin Slice of Anxiety, Avant Appalachia, Shot Glass Journal, Hidden Peak Press, Press, Pause, Press, Red Eft Review, Tickets to Midnight, Vol.3, Ranger Magazine, Fine Lines, The Fib Review*

Special thanks to Mark McClane and Tony Hayden and the whole OAC gang.

Abraham Smith: Smith wishes to thank the Ozarkian Quixote Society for this lucky chance to constellate and bray.

John Dorsey: *Chaos, Solitary Plover, Impspired* & the *Ucity Review.*

Thanks is given to the editors as well as the board and staff of Osage Arts Community, where these pieces were created.

Justin Hamm: *The Rumpus, Pine Hills Review*

TABLE OF CONTENTS

Jason Ryberg

Abraham Smith

John Dorsey

Justin Hamm

...and when there was no meat, we
ate fowl and when there was no fowl, we ate crawdad
and when there was no crawdad to be found,
we ate sand.

-Anonymous Convict,
Maricopa County Maximum
Security Correctional Facility
For Men, State Farm Road
Number 31, Tempe, Arizona

And When There Was No Crawdad, We Ate Sand

Jason Ryberg

Jason Ryberg is the author of twenty-two collections of poetry, six screenplays, a few short stories, a box full of folders, notebooks and scraps of paper that could one day be (loosely) construed as a novel, and countless love letters (never sent). He is currently an artist-in-residence at both The Prospero Institute of Disquieted P/o/e/t/i/c/s and the Osage Arts Community, and is an editor and designer at Spartan Books. His work has appeared in *As it Ought to Be, Up the Staircase Quarterly, Thimble Literary Magazine, I-70 Review, Main Street Rag, The Arkansas Review* and various other journals and anthologies. He lives somewhere in the Ozarks, near the Gasconade River, with a rooster named Little Red and a Billy-goat named Giuseppe.

The White Light of Universal Upload, Etc., Etc.,

I think, before I die, I'd like to live in a lighthouse,

    for a while, or maybe a succession of lighthouses

(if I plan this thing out just right), right up to that point,

    I guess, where they carry me out in a bag, hopefully

not too long after a final glass of something

    ridiculously expensive and some final moment

of clarity where the soul and

    the synapses are, at last, fused together

with the white light of universal up-

    load, etc., etc., But please, no bleak burial at

sea for me, thank you, but instead,

    maybe the seed of

a Pear or

    Cherry

tree

    sewn

up

    in

my rib

    cage and an

old burlap sack for

    a shroud, then bury me in a

shallow grave on a lonely, wind-swept hill somewhere or

    right next to a winding creek, and let the seasons

do their thing (if the coyotes don't, first).

Tin Cup Lightning

There's tin cup lightning
in the sky and a tiny
distant music is
 floating upriver from some-
 where (Buck Owens or George Jones?).

And When There Was No
Crawdad, We Ate Sand

An

      old

            postcard

of William

      Burroughs sitting in

            a folding chair, holding a bull-

whip in one hand and a cane in the other (rumored

      to house a sword that was routinely sharpened,

            no doubt), his weathered Stetson fedora

jauntily cocked on his head, a thin smile and a look

      in his eye that, for some reason,

            made me think of the

old Arab

      proverb:

            There
            are
            no
            signs
            in the
            desert that
            read "Do Not Eat Sand."

Blue Light

No moon or stars out
tonight, only the blue light
of televisions
flickering in living room
    windows, up and down the street.

Um, Goldman Sachs?

It
all
started
with a BANG,
BANG, BANG at the door
and it's 7 o'clock in the
morning on a Saturday, which, I only do, these
days, for $30 an hour (or more)

    but really would prefer not to do at all
when 8 or 9 or even 10 is such a more

       reasonable and civilized hour to haul one-self

       up from the deep wishing well of dreams, like
you were some kind of recently reanimated corpse

    that must have been violently
dispatched and hastily disposed of only the night
before, now rudely disturbed to
find what can only
be described
(kindly,
of
course),
as
a
gaggle
of dowdy
and bovine old gals
standing on your porch, asking you,
(free of irony): *Sir, do you know who rules the world?*

Where the Light Barely Reaches

for Mark Hennessy

All our names are scrawled
in the manifest and locked
away in the hold
    of a sunken ship somewhere
on the floor of the ocean,
    where the light barely reaches.

Men of Roughly Hüsker Dü
Era Appropriateness

An
old
blue truck
with a black
origami crane
hanging from the rear-view mirror

hisses down a slick, small town street, upon which a thin
sheath of ice has been slowly forming all day,

beneath a cold, sunless sky of clouds that
look like pillow stuffing. And an old cassette tape-deck
is reeling out Hüsker Dü's *Zen Arcade* into the
super-heated air of the cab,

where three men of roughly Hüsker Dü era
appropriateness hoist hand grenades of
Mickey's Big Mouth Malt Liquor in the dashboard's glow, while
singing along as best as they
can remember to
songs they once
had burned
in-
to
their
brains.

Passing Truck

How many lifetimes
ago did that passing truck
    cause the coffee in
your cup to ripple, the plates
    in the cupboard to rattle?

The Conversations of Ghosts

Sometimes I'd swear that
the ancient box fan I've hauled
    around with me for
    years is a receiver for
    the conversations of ghosts,

not unlike the way
hat's I've bought at vintage shops
    still hold trace elements
    of the residual thoughts
    of their previous owners.

Memos

It would seem the old,
leathery lizard of the
hind-most part of our
    brain, down in its sub-sub-base-
    ment, is still receiving all
    our inter-office memos.

A Morning Sky, Dark
and Alive with Fissures and
Fault Lines of Lightning,

yellow wildflowers
in a ditch by the side of
a two-lane country

highway, a red-tailed
hawk perched on a telephone
pole, a butterfly

resting on a fence
post, slowly opening and
closing its x-ray

blue wings as thunder
begins to grumble up from
its deep primeval

pumps and bellows, and
the first few drops of rain hit
the hot, cracked tarmac.

Miles above, an old
satellite goes about its
cold, lonely business.

Washed Away

Cracks in a windshield
make maps for forgotten roads
    and shortcuts home that
were washed away years ago
    by floods from the ancient world.

Cop Cars on the Distant Horizon

The clouds are rubbing
the moon's bald head and wiping
his tears as they pass,

and the darkness all
around us is haunted by
the ghosts of hobos

and highway men, just
as the fossils of ancient,
prehistoric sharks

and whales vibrate and
call to us across time from
their resting places,

and a black cat bone
is hanging by a guitar
string from a rear-view-

mirror, in which an
old house, alive and dancing
with flames and sparks and

the bright flashing red
lights of fire trucks and cop cars
can be seen on the

distant receding
horizon as the news comes
on the radio.

Short Stories

Cherry-red cop lights
   flashing at the heart of an
old foggy inner-
    city cemetery full
      of too many short stories.

Tinfoil Stars Above a Street Corner Scene

Night

is

staging

its puppet

show full of tinfoil

stars above a street corner scene

in some nameless AnyHowTown, USA, where-in

an organ grinder and his prancing, prat-falling

monkey are being served papers by

a drunken homicide detective (who's clearly

fallen on hard times (his dreams of a better life

buried deep in old ammo boxes at

the bottom of a lake full of drowned trees

and sunken rowboats)), but it's not until the

third act that it's revealed that the smiling, goat-footed

balloon man, apparently, keeps

detailed dossiers

on each one

of us

and

paints

his

hooves

a different

color every-

day, depending on how he feels.

Broken Fiddle

Tonight, the moon is
    a white chrysanthemum and
a lone cricket is
squeaking out a sad country
        tune on a broken fiddle.

Reconsider

Long is the night slept in a dank old tool shed
     with nothing but an old-school army cot,
          a kitchen table, a chair and a Coleman electric lamp
hanging down from a rafter on
     the end of a strap.
The cracking
     and crash
          of

a

     tree

          limb

     now and

               then, plus the
     odd call and response
               of two or more mysterious
     creatures out there and what absolutely had to have
been a twig snapping, nearby, might just
               make you reconsider your position on guns.

Super-Max

Red rooster strutting
    about the backyard like it
was a super-max
    detention facility
and all the hens, his bitches.

A Certain Cloud

Who
   would
      have thought
         that a bike
  left standing next to
    a tree in the woods, who knows how
many decades ago, would now find itself wrapped-up
    and encased in its trunk, twenty some-odd feet
      off the ground, as if grasped by some woodland
giant and held up to the sky as a sort of prize
   in its attempt to win-over
     a certain cloud that
it's had its
      eye and
    mind
      on
    for
     some
       time, now?

Knucklebone

Outside the moon is
a knucklebone and someone
   is staging a post-
post-modernist production
    of *Our Town* in the old black
     box theater of my dreams.

But, Then Again

The moon is grieving
behind a cloud for a star
that has fallen from

universal grace,
and moths are twirling around
the front porch light like

Sufi Dervishes,
and sheets left out all night on
clotheslines in the back-

yard are billowing
like ghosts in the wind, and some-
where, off in the woods -

the sound of what you'd
swear was a tree suddenly
cracking and falling

under the weight of
all that time and stillness, but
then again, you can't

remember if you've
ever actually heard
a tree fall in the

woods, but you're sure
none of the ghosts you've seen looked
anything like that.

Out Here

Underground rivers
of memory, country grave-
yards of secrets; out
    here, the winters are always
    old black and white photographs.

My Own Personal Underworld

apologies to Lester Raymer

It

would

seem he's

part soldier,

harlequin and high

trapeze artist, this guy, I mean,

who visits me in my dreams, sometimes, like my very

own personal Virgil, giving me the first class

guided tour through what appears to be

my own personal underworld (that, while not being

particularly hellish, by

any means, still has

a kind of

moody,

weird,

old

late,

late

movie

atmosphere

about it, as it

plays out beneath a circus tent,

let's say, stitched together from

silk bed sheets and night gowns,

within the ruins of an old gothic cathedral

full of strangely calm black chickens.

Walkin' Boss

for Thad Haverkamp

On days like this (one
hundred-plus in the shade and
no breeze), the sun is
a mean walkin' boss with a
    loaded cane, mirrors for eyes
    and a big dog on a chain.

Origin Stories

There's
    a
   black snake
  in the tall
       grass, a crow in the
     ribcage of a Willow tree, and
some of the old gods have been seen, reportedly, out
   walking the cornrows at dusk, whispering about
        this and that; meanwhile, I'm just sitting
here, sipping a bitter tea brewed from cemetery
    grass, making up stories about
  the origins of
    a Russian
       nesting
     doll
  that
   has
     washed
   ashore,
      somehow, on
  the muddy banks of
      the mighty Gasconade River.

Abraham Smith

Abraham Smith was raised around Ladysmith, Wisconsin, and lives along the Wasatch Front, where he is associate professor of English and co-director of Creative Writing at Weber State University. His most recent poetry collection is *One Warm Morning* (Stubborn Mule Press, 2025). Away from his desk, Smith improvises poems inside songs with the Snarlin' Yarns: thesnarlinyarnsut.bandcamp.com.

BLUR-T

AND there are refs
runnin backwards
in our day heads see
left hand counting
gym sneakers squeaking
sweat uncomplicated by habits
it's dawn bird chirp it's dark bird cheap
AND the nests squeeze
a little lean to the east
sandwich masoned with love
lifted on average 7 times see
there's one tooth to the taste
AND there's one light
in the house hall lit milk wilt blue
dragon spine bone
dragon spine bone special
shines like an onion
fresh pulled dirt shook
heart of the snow acts the curtain
man with unplanned hair
speaks like he sleeps see
with a mouthfulla dart cork
AND hwy carrion issue shoes
AND there's this bear see
driest bear ever eating and eating
packing peanuts cranes on sky
open it see bored dead easy

no video games in heaven
mushroom for a next life
right up out of the soggy ground
toad for a heart toad upon a woodchip
AND a spring peeper
in one eye socket
if it's convenient look away
AND rustheart robin sings
phew burbank milkmaid few
mirror hurt u choose
medium shirt free yr spirit media hurt
fear it parrot media hurt beer mirror you you
sparkle wrinkle bury merits turd
beer mirror me screw it jared media hurt
marry yr city seven u in it
sewer anyone?? clean up yr clearing!!
clean up yr plate ingrate meteor hurt
dress up the milkpaid hands free
meow meow care hands free
beer spirit me and her
bluebird media wink wink
many a beauty chevrolet puttputt
beer mirror Thessaly
here meathead here squirrel braille thrill
unique meteor meet meat
here we go meteor bluebird here
seek weird piers in twos iceskirts flirt
skin skinny pocket cut it out right now
diamondmind socksocket
AND rustheart robin brings

eerie sparrow fledfled tinderbird scram

eerie sparrow fightfight

redbirdbluebird seek beauty right here

wink wink meow meow

garret parrot downtown arrow

area yer rite there stamina query legit

bluebird seek weird berry heat

beauty here bluebird here

bite nice grr elite meteor

pilfery filthy delete yr starin

free yr spirit media hurt

beer mirror get it

media herd free yr spirit

meek yurt burbank milkmaid

the papers the straws come in

dyin against feet anything but dogs

loyal and chance buried by the hwy

if there's a dark bark left in them bones

yes woof grr figures yes

in each right tight red berry

robins and waxwings get bombed on

AND half in the bag

sled the wind on a piepan tv tray

you might get 9 rides

you might get 10

never eleven them

rhymes piece too easy

back in the day a nail got nosed

by a hammer

AND i see that we are each

given a choice
a choice chance to follow this way
or turn toward the fences
the ditches the fences
enough wool on us to make it over
AND the broad field
castor moving on the spoon
toward the cramping late day light
those sunglasses lost
on the cut moon windowsill
of the improvised outhouse
out back the dead gas station
were meant for someone
the leprous squintin armadillo sips
from the pothole slobbed full of ozona rain
not one seed in one heat crack unwilling
AND the sound of the dillo taking all that wet in
dragonfire broach
i draw ears on jaws until everything is floating
up top on toward the lower
let your weight laugh polite at wait
AND drifting bump the bottom
AND softly cereal box full of silty water
somewhere in the fridge
from over the border
in illinois a factory
whiter than what the dentists
try and sell you
AND it was a ghost farm ghost
AND stones swore an oath for forgetting

only what gives when pressed against
remembers the number
of times the heart kept dirty
in whip tip tail nest watching cat
borrows a name where she can
with toothpicks with fish bones
when froze mink milk melts
thicker down the incisor
did you just paint the lightswitch to on
yes i did do no apologies
to the tv aquarium
brain afloat like a kidney in a toaster
AND those are rob file's piranhas
aren't they yes sir killer fish
have a way of keeping time
by circling don't let that 11thumb drunk try
try asking living wine to calm down
no happiness in joy they say
or is that just me
misremembering the misfit's
decree again turkey feet marks all over
their cute lean pineapple knife shadows
run the otter mop belly
with the motion of firehoses
made of hippo tripes
AND scoop the light places
to shell wheel skins in
knot part ways bow loose
 weak ass plant currency
arizona in a hurry to bogey

the par 666 thistleseed loner bones
milkweed matchsticks
packed jut like a cousin
later for lifer fork shush luncheon
soft fence under share softer
the dog dug it go gone nation back
spring flood logic man
the soft flatters and the hard matters
in this way swamp lap hospitality
us and teacher raise cupped palms
of romantic dirt to sky
the sounds of the young aspens
moving stirring the wind sound
of my knee going down
AND this snowmelt from shook pines
visines in my right eye
post heel cool needle depot
at the same moment others of it
sleep in the creek sleeps in the creek
only trucks this time of year
unafraid of hard work
who here isn't in on
what we talked out
all that nite by wet fart alone
talk about arrival at understanding
digging potato in the rain
get anything flat enough
AND you got a runner up to the slip-n-slide
drop the deerhoof on the record
AND the frog faces stamplick time

a hundred thousand

stuck tongues a touch frozen

strange taste school pole spine

one by one loosen

oldtimer in the grocery line

pickin deliberate

a dollar a dime

innocent stoop concrete

carries a mayonnaise jar

like a glass hand thick

with cigarette butt toes

i see so many things

i don't know the meanings of

i know you do too

to be pierced

again again by things

let's admit the mind

is a limber nest

in a drawer in a museum

bombed as afterthought

AND when cranes land

they land like kites

AND they land like airplanes

AND they land like old people

tiny legs shamaning the water slide

could a dog get hurt snorting dust

from a badger hole

is that what they call the bad dust there

why does the sound of construction

strike us as a pain in the ass but the sound

of hundreds of thousands of cranes
feels like eating coupons
legdrag spectral cake clock again
yes they moved a house
by burying a log upright
AND with the horses and with ropes
anything can be done
is time a circle of piranha juice
what's learned from
your own feet in yr own tracks
see they were both going a time
the same way and i suppose
life by its richer communions
it's fine to say we went along
the same way a time
AND a clock's made of circles
so it'll fit in a room faces work same
AND the blind eye
of this long walk of water
what's justice
come see heart's mouth
drunk on blood
AND the mouth heart
of truth antlered with gibbons
of light and wind emotion meaning
saying what you are really feeling
to and thru crow nest rough deletions
rabbit rabbit rabbit rabbit
cribbage derangements
rabbit rabbit rabbit rabbit

tastes of days stacked like grains of wood
oblong in the legs of the easel and lingering
to thank the sandwich twice seven vines
thank savage sage after rain
no deal big it meant
nothin to me thank flat tire soap chicory
thank the rivering road
good arm to the elbow out the window
under raven eddies
the hips of the thermals
give sound of pulling
an xray apron thru a keyhole
dust doubling your eyebrows
the caterpillars
eat the leaves of your eyes while you sleep
leave little lines
bored kids on desks
like the iceskaters used to
the old basswood in new wind
sounds like sleeping bag zipper
hot coffee in the pot
black as a new tire hot cinnamon
rolls the dough cut with a string
arisen browned melting
flower faces made of summer skin
dale earnheardt captain beefhart har har
hey some sweets need stretchin
hey wednesday can be saturday ez
hardest thing in life to learn is
steer with the hair below your knee some

whatever it is let it
the heart this third foot
never quite reaches
softcroft dreamgreen ground
unless death or love in later spring yet
gotta be going now candy boat snail
bloodspitpink kerosene
right there is something weak
enough to trouble in love
right there's old salt pillar
a compass a cup a grater
keep these three around your neck
or casual sidle up all bologna knee casual
AND the tongue is the flag of the heart
or flagging or windfire
AND take and lick
old loomy salty salt stick
scratches allergic eyes
back of the head
hearth and heart an outhouse on
certain steady stirring sparking steel
AND the stare a hole in
haybales birds sing out
notice my drugs or else
god fallen some chews on them
lower rungs some until they don't taste
times this lowslung turkey
walks me by the eye
clocks me i should shade
turkey whose first foot's

a faithful cactus fail
for i am giant with love
or i am ditty as dirt
with hurt we said at the same
time sun put the flooder
in the game and all the kids
ran random falling with chairs
AND kicking drinks and all
of them that strolled
should have sauced the wing
i never really got a handle on
the ruler except to stir the paint
re-mood the room remember
how dangerous that metal edge was
in the puckering glands
love tensions us by 3's
remember numbers change
with the light through the window we
get to bickering over
the difference between
hayseed and hickory
re-pinchpot drool
these cloverfur roads stray
doses syrup supposes
carbon radios foam cross
nerf toss hug huge
hold on priest's bare
wire nerves stir drinks
with shakes little
earthquakes in

the birdhouse of his
bard owl bowel
banana skins where the hand
towels should be confession ration
tossed together silt pimple hill
ages before eyes vole action probably
saturday brandyy drrunk
this wed ash mornin still
AND birches rise
like strings of snots
from ghosts you can tell it
by their thru the straw voices
drink too much milk
the grocery cart full of pigeons
stepping around ideas for fire
in on 5 then 3 breaking
cheesy crackers and resolute cellophane
only true pictures are those where
folks don't know they are
bein pictured which is why
these days are so lonely everybody doin the splits
on a firework alone in their bedroom on the porch
strained and hollowed as done fireworks
if ever i have a child i'll name her dirt
or hammocks rotted by rain
after the party it's time
to die a little wondering what was
said and if spoon reflects it
does that make knife enough itself
to do a quick nondominant hand

sketch of spruces in oregon
son ya musta been raised
on shrimp shells
willow as this one is going
the daisies erasers
of the sun smell like rub and rub
AND rub the yellow answer
is the ladder with snakes for rungs
some harmless garters
move like living on snot for a day
anybody can do it in the morning
few can thru the night
somewhere in the noon tension of your jaw
is the turtle awake walking
has twilight on a little yarn chain
size of the nettle's shoo need
under the gate through the fern
over the ivy into the pond
staggered with runoff
fever to the touch
spaghetti squash
cryin mama out to yr ballcap killed hair
climb barter bed wet
morning star fruit debt
seed for a stem the usual play
AND this steer circle
shined to a premise
with steaming hunks of cheese
you know you know it
when ya dream fingers teats

whole town no posted speed

the gutters gunnin wide

AND yr life in full in

the little dry reptile eye

stone rollin blind inside

the coach's whistle

goes and moonlights

inn the ref's

AND clear over 100 some bones in you

get to writing this poem out

long hand wide white letters

for the children of the firemen

the poles they jump to concrete

AND red trucks it's important

kept frictionless keep

with little mouse couches

of herring for the oiling

pickled will pit things in time

surface says to worship depth

fresh mess always

blocky robot flesh eyes

pileateds going long

for slumber stoned winter ants

by morse for apnea

a light to read by

nearer apple haunter

every used car

of my long life

wouldn't start

c'mon hopeless cart

sucker bought it
without the crucial belting wheel
AND did you ever notice folks
get more harried and frequent and urgent tryin
won't startle on either
of the 9 tries clasped
in the perfume bottle
of the titmouse body
sneerers look out
the past is a high dung hill
swept clean by the windy
flame of living i see seeing
i am set free from everything
save trying to match the body
with the song all the trees
pinned with socks
full of talkin sun look thru
at the cutup fish
titmice jelly grey
they keep a little apricot
along the brief blade of themselves
AND it's good rictus litmus
you don't trust nobody didn't grow up
with their family car maybe starting maybe not
it was one way to cultivate the beautiful hope muscle
call me indecisive but i grew my i am
sitting in the back seat of maybe wait a minute
then try again
overing firework the woodcock
goofy drool for a beak

whose body the ground

whistles away badminton midsummer

don't freak out it's just a game

last year's oak leaf

three actually superimposed

AND slicked thru with snowmelt

winter pressure like the machine

makes the dimes

fish gut slim slime

AND thin the color of going is

close to nothing

the dirt is a mouth without a face

AND it's hard not to think of life

as popcorn flowering hard

some just burnt

tough as rock

used to pick for dollar a day

AND gone

tho that ditch remains

for the spring water to run

AND does it

while the movie plays

AND dad snores

in his chair of dirt

rocking only

when few bear left

still step firm

say it all to lake superior

the shore ice shuddering

to sleep at the pace of sleep

stacked hectic morass

jalousies jerked by methheads

say the truth about who you were

AND are days like distances

then immediate as a cut finger

to the bald fuses of lemon juices

frozen then sodden

the freezer bag leaking

then hard and almost unfelt

as a glazed blue bowl

into which is dropped

a bellyflopping penny

lincoln's lips making dove

while the ringing in your ears

AND the shimmying mossy coin

ink a deal to sell twistyties to

diving boards inside whose

long green tongue jangles

old charm bracelets

AND friendship bracelets

the roller skate and frog

yes the pines' thousand little

frog pins and fishbone bristle odes

erase the sound and usher it

as i understand

there are around 17 ways

to say oh and o

this way to towel your seat

this chevy cave is made for creeps

AND cripes for polite christ

whose back was a loggin road
of splinters and sicksweet
sawdusts on each rides
a fat man in a cartoon
on a camel at a fair
he's missing what's behind
him lion on two feet
whose walkin coffin boxy xray shows
a heart draped in cokebottle glasses
moused clear circular clear
with elbow steamers
with floursack underwear
gradual the vista real
live like a lion lives
within reason
there's a long car coming
in wind in pines
who is it you don't know don't know
long have you been waiting
for the drawing of an eye
in shape of frozen ice
spidering on your shoulder
that ocean karaoke thing
that hwy on a feather thing
do that jetengine in a sling
that stonebeat shirts thing
breathed thru while the movie dries
yes a sudden downpour at the drive-in
turns your popcorn to
slaughteryard eyes sky and road

share a fishgut grey forever
AND the young hawk
up top the pole
leans like a drunk
on a bar stool
old drunk guy
bird legs
AND this leaning
the past in the front
seat of the head
a quarter a bowl
full of chili
in the nose
redder beak okayed by dusk
AND all the folks say
he says
you can hear the barns
step lower
like elephants onto their knees
there's just this little fizzing crackle on the wind
rice krispies in the mouth
of a methhead
then lucy the parthound otters from
the rain creeked ditch chewing
a drowned mouseratmouse
knows if she stops
i'll suggest don't
runs and chews and chews and runs
if you eat four legs and you
already have four does that give

a temporary eight
spidery turning radiance
not even a ballplayer
with a baseball of tobacco
exploding his right cheek is
graceful as this and i can see his
dentist springing up
in bed from a dream
of statues ankle deep in a fountain
spitting blood and his daughter
placing her lips to the face of one
god coming away with a mouthful
dad it's only wine it's only war merlot
AND the ballplayer
he's making a killing forgetting
his last mistake and this dentist
head shakes like a rainy horse
into the cold side of the pillow the smaller bones
turning in the concrete mixer
of lucy's mouth seconds
from where i soon am
AND suddenly i feel i feel them
bones like seconds
clock leg drag
burnt pizza mouth
we are talkin
medium bad about
the person when
the person walks in
AND the mouseturd long

mosquito full of turtle blood
rests satisfied older
on the right side
of the screen
nodding along to
stackable rhythms and
pollen slips
hung over shower racks
at the livin dead bottom
of old pond ignore
sounds like sweepin
the floor with a dead chicken
i meant the clicking
bones of the windfuss winded kite
we are a lot to bear i know heehee
this motel has way how many
wormy apples
gave the deer the runs
for lightbulbs and there are
rooms on rooms
only countable
by how many times
the chasing dog
twitches and shivers
in dreams in all reality
these bloods yours mine
lean to looser grapes in bears
the party buses fulla saints
takin deeper pulls
from each other's toes

one day the silty dirt

stood up

own two feet situation

went the bird route became crane

cranes crane the field they shapelier the sky they

stand like a war soldier graveyard so many so close

we count with our heart count on it

no they weren't

the idea for the peace sign

yes they were how forks came about

by the way they were the big kite idea

AND the ramones out back of

the club leaning and smoking thin

enough to be nothing at all tall

enough to be it all to be everything see

i let next month's ants take my words

the river says i am frowning

but the river can only repeat after me backwards

the heart it's a shame with a certain stetho

goes drama drama drama drama

in the jello i see suspended little

unseen sound is sweetest shetlin

ya can't ride can only walk beside

my song prayer dead ringer

no one's coyote

knows every sad one

about the stranger's

horseshoe ringing tailbone

donkeyed to the trash

bearded door whittled skinny

this kin skin thin how
by walking just outside
banana cream pie sore
circles of search light
free onion's not
the only anything
you pick pickup ford green
there's real dead
AND there's antler shed dead
AND there's meteor hand flight
meteor hand flight beaconite
AND there's hotel loam shawl
hotel loam sticky shawl
a sorrel shower of worms
inclined to move for
love works to outwit robin
inclined to rock wooden
for love works to tipple
death's parttime drizzle living
doubledutch AND i am forgetting
for the children
their wee hands in trust twists
the very best parts
kissy face tungsten chagrin hearts
prickle in and you ride out from them
a sudden sudden gut gut
of highways loose
AND the soul is a tiny toy car
bloodlet fruit rollup onramp
remember laws

broken by breath bend back around
sit with a cup of tea
fogs the window good to draw on
single pane you can
hear everything
the junco feet feeling like closing
around the dead pine in time do
yes when it's raining like this
on june 11th
raining like the dream
of the methhead
acupuncture specialists
the methheads they don't come out
AND the catalytics they grin
snug smug as the prostate
of those young in the morgue
ah but the turtles
the alligator snappers do rise
cut from a time
when you needed combat gear
to toadfoot clawrut lowstooldrag
pond to pond turtle potholes by morning
did you bring your own bags
under your eyes
kevlar eyelids to grab some ziplocs
AND lipton's for sun tea their tails lining
the gravel road dust
in snake switchbacks
tap tap wet wet what's tough's loosening
dig in at edges and line the lips

of the road with eggs round as
saying same thing at the start
AND end wail in whimper out
or whimper in wail out
a little of both i am guessing
AND always always that hospital light
AND i was born to sing bears
fresh feather stomp underwears
chosen range name squint
fair and free prelude to openin the eyes
they just go on everywhere really
AND when we die our shadows trunk
group and grappa there in bear
AND deer is the horse
only ghosts can ride
like a taxi you can tell it when
the tail is on the rise see
ghosts ride backwards
that's them holding on
to page rages of smokes
other sides of the panes
the cranes journey
AND i lift my chin like a crane
AND i hear the wind of them
somewhere between creak
and whistle sound of tree water
gettin knotty my mouth open
as a shovel
the dirt of me
going
gah

John Dorsey

John Dorsey is the former Poet Laureate of Belle, MO. He is the author of several collections of poetry, including *Which Way to the River: Selected Poems: 2016-2020* (OAC Books, 2020), *Sundown at the Redneck Carnival,* (Spartan Press, 2022), *Pocatello Wildflower,* (Crisis Chronicles Press, 2023) and *Dead Photographs,* (Stubborn Mule Press, 2024). He may be reached at archerevans@yahoo.com.

Telegrams from a Chicken's Neck

leroi jones died today
long pauses of morning
my clean laundry
hidden in loneliness
your tent of reason
in the name of charity

my father did it
for the glory
of regrets

we all have a cold
the alarm
doesn't give a damn.

Billie Holiday of the Burning Sky

billie holiday of the drifting light
struck dumb by the sea of love
burning through sad long days
roots of spring demons
the heart of sunlight
softly singing.

The Lord of Pity & Barbed Wire

is not far away
the moonshine resurrection
of agony
piled high
yesterday
the air
blew jazz songs
from a dead church.

Henry Miller is Afraid

beloved hillbillies
of ageless lips
took their time
whispering common lines
to god.

Wild Places of Wet Daggers

the last breath
of floating leaves
gloom is tradition
flown away
to never never land
open your lungs
& let out your song
of the never ending night
of the burning stars
hiding little things
that gather
like ashes.

A Piece of Pie

a half bottle of scotch
moonlight you drank in autumn air
stars that look
like crumbs.

A Dancing Girl in the Garden of Eden

words falling from her mouth
her big eyes
like drunk christmas trees
the birth of her body
catching the sunlight
pale-faced
& small
vibrating
in the air.

The Panorama of Her Fingers

her tiny body
waist deep in water
an orange blossom
falling into the sun
her soul dangles
her red hair burns.

Shelving Books

sherwood anderson hidden
behind mystery
your tired hands work
in the sunlight.

Drive Recklessly

over the backroads of desire
watch quietly
as we move
through the sky
like secrets.

Morning Love & Rolling Hills

dark in my throat
bodies swung open
into the dance
of revolving doors.

Serious Birds

i hear the sky singing
the song of destiny
in the blood red moonlight
i dance
& the air
leaves my hands.

A Morning Rose

dead automobiles
nearly every morning
an unhappy wind
ate our last memory.

Errol Flynn's Favorite Bar

very old men
would be dead within months
that winter everyone
behaved crazy
everyone relived
his death.

Joel McCrea

girls ignite boys
with honest intentions
ida lupino wanted a match.

Mary Lou's Flowers

are beautiful
like a snake
writing poems.

The Dead Return

to avoid
bad weather.

Babe Ruth in India

buddha gunned down
in 1955.

Nelson Algren had a
Two Year Old Daughter

& kept his head crunk
a loaded shotgun
outside the window
he stole a car
& died two weeks later.

Bind Us Together Sweet Georgia Brown

an old wine bottle
thighs too tired
to curse god
lovers dangling
somewhere beneath
the sky.

Rabbits Chase the Roman Candle

children's endless universe
my organic whisper
the sun illuminating your back
don't forget to sing
a midnight song
of sorrow.

I Was a Kid

a different person
carrying my name
a valid passport
with no place to stay
twenty-five years later in paris
in photos
with no guitar.

October's Skull

springs from a tree
long dead
the moon
kicks my stomach
in the midwestern sun.

Lorine of Quiet Fury

a solitary breeze
with frenzied hands.

Richard Hugo Time Warp

in 1976
you pound your fist
on a table
& divide a river
into living
or dead things

today
somehow
things feel different
the mail just sits there
sunlight scattered
on the ground.

Justin Hamm

Originally from the flatlands of central Illinois, **Justin Hamm** now lives near Twain territory in Missouri. He is the author of five full-length collections of poetry, *O Death, Drinking Guinness With the Dead: Poems 2007-2021*, *The Inheritance, American Ephemeral,* and *Lessons in Ruin;* six poetry chapbooks; and a book of photographs entitled *Midwestern.* He is also the creator of Poet Baseball Cards and the founding editor of the *museum of americana.*

Went To See the Gypsy

"People are going to say, 'Well, [Tempest is]
not very truthful. But a songwriter doesn't
care about what's truthful. What he cares
about is what should've happened, what
could've happened. That's its own kind of truth."

-Bob Dylan, *Rolling Stone*, August 16, 2012

In July of 2013 some friends and I happened to meet a
certain future Nobel Laureate in the parking lot of a
relatively cheap hotel in Peoria, Illinois. This is, you know,
what happened that afternoon. Sort of.

-JH

1.

You know what? He was taller than I expected, despite
what everyone always says—taller, and a lot more
enthusiastic about planting trees. Like two Johnny
Appleseeds we left the tour buses behind and strode out
for barren pastures. He was a fast walker. Purposeful
strides. He pledged to adopt the highways we crossed,
every last one of them, and I said prayers for the roadkill,
just to fill the air with noise besides traffic. The day was
cloudless, the sun a giant egg yolk in the sky. He stopped
and wiped his brow with a calico handkerchief, adjusted
his aviators. We were somewhere lost on the prairie and it
was time to plant the pine cones and anoint them, which
we did without speaking. One of them immediately grew
into a jukebox, another into Shakespeare. You might say
that was when all the fun began.

2.

Right from the first, he seemed oddly preoccupied with salmon. Everything was salmon this and salmon that. Rubbing his thin mustache and muttering to himself over and over. He barely noticed us. All I wanted was an autograph, perhaps a handshake. But he wanted to know why nature would make a fish that had so much trouble mapped out ahead of itself just for the purpose of reproduction. He seemed to both wonder and already know the answer at the same time. Underneath his hoodie and his baseball cap his face sweated in the midsummer heat. His unmistakable nose twitched a little and he rubbed at it in a very idiosyncratic, folk-rock-poet sort of way. Then he lifted his aviators so we could see the squint of his unmistakable blue eyes. They were positively biblical, and also—what's the word?—unmistakable. *Well?* he said, and began tapping his foot on the pavement, as if keeping time to a song. *There must be some kind of an answer to this devilish riddle. I'm waiting.*

3.

There was a jetpack strapped to his back. Otherwise, he looked just how everybody describes him when he's in his public disguise: hoodie, even in the heat; hip-hop length shorts; socks pulled up to his knees. Baseball cap and aviators, the ones he wore when Obama put the Medal of Freedom around his neck on C-SPAN. It was clear this was a man who did not wish to be noticed, unless of course it was for wearing a jetpack. I myself had never seen a jetpack in real life, but I was afraid to allude to it. What if he was offended? So I pretended not to notice. I think he was having some fun at my expense. He kept making what I thought were oblique references. He talked about hoping the new record would "take off" soon, just "rocket up the charts." Just before we parted ways he said it was time he "jetted on out of there." If he was putting me on, his face betrayed nothing. It was immutable. It looked like a holy carving made from ancient stone.

4.

Come to think of it, we were in a bar. It wasn't even a hotel parking lot. I came in wearing a John B. Stetson hat, and there was some kind of a ruckus, one terrible fight. Maybe he liked my John B. Stetson hat and said he wanted it. Maybe I said he couldn't have it. His gun came out. I told him about my family, my wife and the little baby we'd named after him. He made a sneer down below that pencil-thin matador's mustache and said not to worry, that he'd take good care of my family. *Oh, you're a bad man, I said. A bad man, Mr. D.*

5.

Then again, maybe I'm the one who had the gun.

6.

I gave him a postcard. He autographed it. I gave him one of his early records. He autographed it. I gave him a record by Justin Bieber. He autographed it. I gave him a two-dollar bill. He autographed it. I gave him a baby shoe. He autographed it. I gave him a copy of *Huckleberry Finn*. He flipped through it for a minute, almost wistfully. Then he autographed it. He autographed our SUV. He autographed my daughter's shadow. He autographed a couple of old beer cans we found in a dumpster. I chewed some bubble gum and blew a big bubble and he autographed that. He autographed my cell phone. He autographed a storm cloud. He even autographed the place in the sky where the moon would be later in the night. *That way,* he said, *it'll look like I autographed the moon when it finally gets here.* Only later, when I tried to read all of his signatures, did I realize he'd been signing everything *Sinead O'Connor.*

7

I'm embarrassed to say we had been watching him all afternoon. He had removed the railing from the hotel entrance and now there were saw horses set up between the tour buses. A welder's helmet hid his face and gave him, from the neck up, the mysterious air of a medieval knight. Near as I could tell he was creating some kind of sculpture of a bird, looked like maybe it might be a raven. In its guts were welded a strange collection of car parts, carpenter's tools, and garden utensils. We kept our distance, not wanting to agitate him in his work, but he called us over. *Help me lift this piece right here,* he said, *so I can weld it in place.* We held the piece and he welded it in a bright ball of sparks. *What are you making?* we asked him when he'd finished. *Oh, this? It's an ark,* he said, and we laughed. Then we stopped laughing because he wasn't laughing. Nor was the dove that swooped down and landed in a beam of light on his shoulder.

8.

I cannot tell a lie, he said. *I chopped down your cherry tree.* I had
never owned a cherry tree, but he seemed to badly want
forgiveness. So I handed him a 7-up and we sat down on the
curb. *Mmm, fizzy,* he said, after a long swallow. Then he began
to sob uncontrollably, his small body jerking like a puppet.
Hey, easy now, I said, and patted him on the shoulder. The hot
hours passed, the sun scorching my bald scalp. We didn't talk
about much of anything, and I never did learn what secret
caused him to hide his face behind those sunglasses. The pain
was just too much to approach. He was radioactive with it.
If you look at the postcard he autographed for me, you can
see where a single fat teardrop landed, right next to "Best
Wishes." Truthfully, I don't like to take it out and look at it
much anymore.

9.

That's not true, either. He laughed almost the whole
time. At least I think he did. Maybe it was just a
particularly jazzy cough.

10.

My four-year-old daughter wanted to meet him. So I introduced her. Soon, talk turned to *The Cat in the Hat.* He bounced from toe to toe like a boxer as he listened. *What troubles me is the fish's stark inability to accept the trickster's role in reestablishing the boundaries within a societal construct,* said my daughter. *Mmm-hmm,* said our new friend, nodding rhythmically, and something intellectual passed between them which excluded me entirely. They are speaking to each other across an alley through open windows to apartments on a higher plane. I'm down below, playing stickball in the streets with the neighborhood boys. Hopefully someone will remember to tell me what I need to know about the world when the time comes for me to know it.

11.

But nothing I've said yet truly describes him physically. First, he was an eel. Then he was a cheetah. Then he was a dolphin, an orangutan, a hyena. His eyes were blue. His eyes were green. His eyes were yellow, his eyes didn't even match. He was dressed like a hippie. He was dressed like a CEO. He was dressed for a steampunk novel. He spoke like a southerner, like a Midwesterner, like a bluesman, a farmer, a professor of soul. He picked my pocket. He gave me a diploma and called it brains, a clock that ticked and called it my heart. He said he couldn't do much for my courage—a man either had that or he didn't. He asked us to please cuff his hands and put him in a large tank of water. He opened his mouth to show us the tiny Lord Byron reclining there with a book in the back near his tonsils. He was shy in the most forward and audacious way. It was afternoon everywhere except in the area immediately surrounding him. There the stars floated freely and it was always one minute past midnight.

12.

It was very dark there in the wooden belly of the horse. Around us the citizens of Troy slept in deathly silence. An hour passed, two hours. Every so often there was a quick spark and the smell of burning tobacco, a pinkish glow, smoke. I kept wanting to check my cell phone to see what time it was, but I wasn't sure how he'd take that.

Listen, this was a great idea, I told him finally. *Really, it was. But what comes next?*

He puffed on his cigarette. The cherry flared and relaxed. *Shit, man, I don't know,* he said. *I never got that far in the book.*

13.

At first, I didn't notice the sixties standing nearby. They were dressed like a social activist, all in black, collective mouth taped closed. There were large ideas and impossible hopes Gorilla-glued to their forehead. It was clear who they deemed to be their master. The sixties were like a puppy dog, a stray sniffing at his tennis-shoed feet, whimpering. I began to feel sorry for the sixties, to wonder if I fed them if they would follow me home. He was, for his part, entirely unmoved, even as they inched their collective wet snout up toward his crotch. Even as they grew increasingly insistent.

14.

His hands were small and his nails were yellow and not well kept. Apparently this was not something he cared much about until I pointed it out to him. Then he became agitated. He began to talk in quick bursts. *I gotta get rid of these hands, man. I just have to. You've gotta trade me hands, that's all there is to it. You've gotta trade me before the show tonight.* So we traded hands. He seemed okay with the trade, but I had no idea what to do with folk-rock poet hands. I supposed I could play some guitar or keyboard with them, or write a pretty mean folk-rock song with poetic lyrics. But all I could think about was how I would have to touch my wife with these hands, and it bothered me. Even in the dark I would know. I happened to look up then and could see the same thought had occurred to him at almost the exact same moment. Somehow, he didn't seem to mind so much.

15.

We were about out of time. In his chest, where his heart should have been, was an hourglass. He unzipped his hoodie three-quarters of the way so we could see this hourglass, which we thought was mighty generous of him. We looked at it, and at each other, and at him, and a whole universe of ideas fell almost but not quite into place, like pieces to a jigsaw puzzle that are close matches but not quite correct, perhaps due to factory defect. Then he zipped his hoodie back up. Afterward, I went home, like anyone would, and set about trying to become a spiritual healer. I laid hands upon broken cookie jars and rustbucket jalopy old Fords, afraid my newfound powers might be too intense for humans. As a child I was a Pentecostal and it was a great disappointment I could never speak in tongues. Now I did so without warning. I also ran a constant fever of 107 degrees. The last moments of our meeting haunted me. I couldn't set it aside. On the ground near his feet, I remember, was a cowboy hat. He bent down and picked it up, dusted it off. Pulled back his hood and removed his baseball cap. The cowboy hat fit nicely on his head of curly gray hair. He wore it and stood there between the tour buses and waited a long time for us to say something—perhaps to pass judgment? Then he turned and strode off through the soupy humidity. I'm certain I'll never forget the purpose in his gait.

Only a Dream

Neil Young wakes in the semidarkness, rises like the very sun itself, and places upon his head a dusty black fedora. He wraps his physical manifestation within a flannel shirt as if wrapping it within a shroud of the Holy Spirit. He eats something organic and picks up the news and quickly puts down the news, and outside is waiting a specially-engineered, environmentally-conscious classic car into which Neil Young climbs with the greatest pleasure.

He stretches, rubs his eyes, keys the ignition.

Neil Young's dreams have been troubling. In them, there was a Rubik's Cube that Neil Young had been trying to solve. This Rubik's Cube should have been called the Devil's Cube, so certain is Neil Young that he could not have solved it, even if he had been given a lifetime. Now, as the American West unfolds before him like a motion picture that does not move but is, rather, moved through, Neil Young begins to mentally design a machine that will not only solve the Rubik's Cube but also punish the Rubik's Cube for being all but unsolvable. Neil Young, in his dream, and in the here and now, as they call it—in "dream" or in "reality"—is suddenly willing to do anything, willing to risk anything to bring this machine to fruition. He will meet presidents and prime ministers. He will go on television and try to remain at least moderately cheerful and accessible. He will record new music, perhaps even alongside fellow rock icons with whom his current relations are rumored to be as frigid as Ontarian winter.

Of course, all of this is a tall order, even for Neil Young, who finds himself suddenly sweating beneath his fedora with the heat of the enormous pressures he places upon himself. Off comes the fedora. The western atmosphere sucks through the car window and swirls around Neil Young's uncapped head, cools him, restores his senses. He wipes his forehead with handkerchief, catches a glimpse of himself hatless in the rearview.

His hair is less substantial than it was at one time. His face is different than he usually imagines it. His eyes still cut, but . . .but . . . but . . .

I look so . . . mortal, Neil Young thinks. Back on goes the fedora, quickly, and yes, Neil Young feels himself again, restored to legend-in-the-flesh status, just another rock god out cruising in his environmentally-friendly land yacht to breathe in the soul of the mountains and the essence of the valleys he so desperately hopes but is not confident will be here for future generations.

He reminds himself the fedora stays where it is from now on.

Now a song begins to knock at the cellar door of Neil Young's imagination. He applies greater pressure to the gas pedal, feels the minutes and the miles falling away like old habits and old friends. Someplace deep and lost and wild, Neil Young pulls over. He takes out, or perhaps conjures up, a guitar and an amplifier, which he plugs directly into the side of the first mountain he reaches. This perhaps seems unlikely, and it would be, except that it happens. It is the truest thing you will find written here. Neil Young plugs the amplifier into the side of the mountain and he plugs the guitar into the amplifier and he makes a contorted face and begins to do Neil-Young-like things to/with the guitar. The sound is the sound of an electric beard trimmer and a concrete truck making strangely melodic love. The sound travels high out over the lands and everything the lands support—

the flowers, the cities, the rivers, the graves of the famous and the graves of the forgotten alike. The sound travels out over everything and everything willingly submits, agrees to believe that Neil Young can create anything Neil Young can dream. The irony: in that same moment Neil Young himself no longer believes. Neither does he disbelieve. He has

no opinion, in fact, no existence except in the noise he has become. Neil Young has forgotten the Rubik's Cube of the long night behind, the punitive measures he wished to take against it, the great promise of his unmade machine.

Our scene must shift now. Missouri. Early morning, just me and a steaming cup of Jamaican blend, three sugars and three creams. I'm sitting at an outdoor table watching the breath steam like dragon smoke from the mouths of the winter sidewalk walkers, Neil Young's memoir spread open beside me, when the sound of his guitar hits my ears. I can't tell if it is real or if it is something I have invented from what I have been reading.

I hear the guitar and soon after I hear the trees calling back. And the mountains, and the valleys, too, and the last clean rivers and a chorus of gleaming fish. And I wonder if these voices are mine. Do they belong to my mind? Or are they formed from the corporeal stuff of this world? That's the thing. I can't begin to say for certain.

For their part, the mountains and valleys and rivers and fish do not seem to care. *Neil Young,* they howl in ragged unison, responding to the call of his guitar, and their howls stretch the long miles between us.

Neil Young. Neil Young. Neil Young.

From *The Autobiography of Mark Twain*

to invent

himself

from

the past centuries

and

the unborn tribe

He made a sudden spring

no: rehearsed

conscious

of   nothing except   escape

From *The Autobiography of Mark Twain*

He lay in a metallic burial case

                                              thinking

I can still feel something

   another boat

   stretched upon a mattress   of

                        physic   s

From *The Autobiography of Mark Twain*

It is very difficult to look

morning after morning
for   carved angels enough
to go on

You *have* to turn your face

away

From *The Autobiography of Mark Twain*

                          American

                                    Suffering

                  will be worth fifty cents

to go and look

come

              do it   write a line or two

cheerfully

From *The Autobiography of Mark Twain*

he got out his revolver   and said
    I have got   a bullet

if you should want to play

                    I did not know

                              blood

        was a reference to
the American

overplus of property

From *The Autobiography of Mark Twain*

But wait a minute

        man is the monkey's superior

             only

              in

      that

        he

           is

a swindle

          without character

From *The Autobiography of Mark Twain*

a   Christian city

doing the best we can

    paying those boys twenty to forty thousand dollars

privately

        we   say

             to   those

boys

          Now then,

each of you   is

                                         sold

This project was made possible, in part, by generous support from the Osage Arts Community.

Osage Arts Community provides temporary time, space and support for the creation of new artistic works in a retreat format, serving creative people of all kinds — visual artists, composers, poets, fiction and nonfiction writers. Located on a 152-acre farm in an isolated rural mountainside setting in Central Missouri and bordered by ¾ of a mile of the Gasconade River, OAC provides residencies to those working alone, as well as welcoming collaborative teams, offering living space and workspace in a country environment to emerging and mid-career artists. For more information, visit us at www.osageac.org

Osage Arts Community